ELI MANNING
Football Superstar

BY MATT SCHEFF

CAPSTONE PRESS
a capstone imprint

Sports Illustrated Kids Superstar Athletes are published by Capstone Press,
1710 Roe Crest Drive, North Mankato, Minnesota 56003.
www.capstonepub.com

Library of Congress Cataloging-in-Publication Data
Scheff, Matt.
  Eli Manning : football superstar / by Matt Scheff.
      pages cm.—(Sports Illustrated kids. Superstar athletes)
  Includes bibliographical references and index.
  Summary: "Presents the athletic biography of Eli Manning, including his career as a high school, college, and
professional athlete"—Provided by publisher.
  ISBN 978-1-4765-8601-4 (library binding)
  ISBN 978-1-4765-9430-9 (paperback.)
1. Manning, Eli, 1981—Juvenile literature. 2. Football players—United States—Biography—Juvenile literature.
3. Quarterbacks (Football)—United States—Biography—Juvenile literature.
I. Title.
  GV939.M2887S35 2014
  796.332092–dc23
  [B]   2013025100

Editorial Credits

Nate LeBoutillier, editor; Lori Bye, designer; Eric Gohl, media researcher; Eric Manske, production specialist

Photo Credits

Newscom: Icon SMI/Sporting News/Bob Leverone, 12; Sports Illustrated: Al Tielemans, cover (all), 2–3, 5, 15, 22
(middle & bottom), Bill Frakes, 9, 22 (top), 24, Bob Rosato, 10, 16, Damian Strohmeyer, 1, John W. McDonough, 6,
Robert Beck, 19, Simon Bruty, 21, 23

Design Elements

Shutterstock/chudo-yudo, designerpix, Fassver Anna, Fazakas Mihaly

Direct Quotations

Page 7, from February 3, 2008, *ESPN* article "Eli, Monster Defense Power Giants to Shocking Super Bowl Victory"
by Greg Garber, www.espn.com

Page 14, from January 11, 2006, *New York Times* article "Manning's Career Could Use an Off-Season Exorcism" by
John Branch, www.nytimes.com

Page 18, from February 5, 2012, *Huffingon Post* article. "Eli Manning Super Bowl MVP: Giants QB Wins 2nd Super
Bowl Most Valuable Player Award" by Howard Fendrich, www.huffingtonpost.com

Printed in the United States of America in North Mankato, Minnesota.

092013   007771CGS14

TABLE OF CONTENTS

CHAPTER 1

SUPER BOWL HERO

The New York Giants trailed the New England Patriots 14-10 in Super Bowl XLII in 2008. With just a minute remaining, Giants quarterback Eli Manning dropped back to pass. Patriot defenders charged at him. Some of them even grabbed his jersey. Manning escaped and spied a teammate. He heaved a long pass.

Wide receiver David Tyree made an amazing catch. He pinned the ball to the top of his helmet! A few plays later, Manning lobbed another pass. Wide receiver Plaxico Burress caught it in the end zone. Touchdown! The Giants took a 17-14 lead. The Patriots couldn't score in the final 29 seconds. Manning and his teammates rushed the field. The Giants were Super Bowl champs.

"It's hard to believe, it really is. The drive at the end, there were so many clutch plays by so many guys. It is an unbelievable game and an unbelievable feeling."
—Eli Manning

CHAPTER 2

FOOTBALL IN THE BLOOD

Elisha Nelson Manning was born January 3, 1981, in New Orleans, Louisiana. His father, Archie, was a star college and NFL quarterback. His older brothers, Cooper and Peyton, played the game too. Eli played basketball and baseball in high school. But he was best at football. He was named 1998 Louisiana Player of the Year.

BIG BROTHER

Eli's older brother Peyton went on to become a star quarterback for the Indianapolis Colts and Denver Broncos. Peyton won a Super Bowl with the Colts in 2006.

The Mannings (left to right):
Cooper, Archie, Eli, and Peyton

Manning accepted a **scholarship** to play football at the University of Mississippi (Ole Miss). It was the same college where his father had been a star quarterback. From 2000 to 2003, he passed for a school-record 10,119 yards and 81 touchdowns. In his final game, Manning led Ole Miss to a 31-28 victory in the Cotton Bowl.

scholarship—money provided for a student's education

THE QUIET ONE

Manning has always been soft spoken. His mother said that he didn't start talking until he was 3 years old. His first word was "ball."

The Mannings on Eli's draft day (left to right):
Peyton, Olivia, Eli, and Archie

The San Diego Chargers picked Manning first in the 2004 NFL **Draft**. But Manning was unhappy. He didn't want to play for the Chargers. San Diego traded him to the Giants. Manning signed a contract worth more than $50 million.

draft—an event at which professional teams select new players

CHAPTER 3

WELCOME TO THE NFL

Manning struggled at first. He played little as a **rookie** in 2004. He became the full-time starter the following season. Manning helped the Giants reach the playoffs in 2005 and 2006. They lost in the first round both years.

"I'm going to work hard, and I'm going to do everything I can do to become a guy who can be a leader of this team. ... That's where I want to be next year."
—Eli Manning after the 2005 season

rookie—a first-year player

The Giants didn't have a great regular season in 2007, but they made the playoffs. They won three straight road games to reach the Super Bowl. Then they shocked the **undefeated** Patriots to win it all. Manning was named Super Bowl Most Valuable Player (MVP).

undefeated—having lost zero games during the season

The Giants lost in the first round of the 2008 playoffs. They missed the playoffs in 2009 and 2010. They went just 9-7 in 2011. But then Manning and the Giants got hot in the playoffs. They advanced to Super Bowl XLVI to face the Patriots. Late in the game, Manning led another game-winning drive. Once again, Manning and the Giants were the champions!

"We knew that we had no more time left. We had to go down and score, and guys stepped up and made great plays."
—Eli Manning on the Giants' game-winning drive in Super Bowl XLVI

CHAPTER 4

MR. CLUTCH

Manning is known for his calm manner. He never gets too excited. That has helped him become a **clutch** player. He seems to play his best when the game is on the line. That ability has helped make him one of the best quarterbacks in the NFL. Giants fans know never to count their team out as long as Manning is their quarterback.

clutch—able to perform one's best in the most important games or situations

TIMELINE

1981—Manning is born January 3 in New Orleans.

1998—Manning is named Louisiana's high school football Player of the Year.

2004—Manning helps Ole Miss to a victory over Oklahoma State in the Cotton Bowl; Manning signs with the Giants after the NFL Draft.

2008—The Giants defeat New England Patriots in the Super Bowl; Manning wins Super Bowl MVP.

2011—Manning leads the NFL by pulling off eight game-winning drives.

2012—The Giants win the Super Bowl, again over New England, as Manning wins a second Super Bowl MVP.

2013—Manning is named to his third Pro Bowl.

GLOSSARY

clutch (KLUTCH)—able to perform one's best in the most important games or situations

draft (DRAFT)—an event at which professional teams select new players

rookie (RUK-ee)—a first-year player

scholarship (SKA-lur-ship)—money provided for a student's education

undefeated (un-dee-FEET-ed)—having lost zero games during the season

READ MORE

Artell, Mike. *Peyton Manning: Football Superstar.* Sports Illustrated Kids. North Mankato, Minn.: Capstone Press, 2012.

Manning, Archie, Eli Manning & Peyton Manning. *Family Huddle.* New York: Scholastic Press, 2009.

Tracy, Kathleen. *Day by Day with Eli Manning.* Hockessin, Del.: Mitchell Lane Publishers, 2011.

INTERNET SITES

FactHound offers a safe, fun way to find Internet sites related to this book. All of the sites on FactHound have been researched by our staff.

Here's all you do:

Visit *www.facthound.com*

Type in this code: 9781476586014

INDEX